Ready to Lead

An Entry Guide for New Principals

Troy Mooney and Herbert O'Neil

Ready to Lead: An Entry Guide for New Principals

Produced April 2017

Troy Mooney

Email: Troy.mooney@lifeschools.net

Twitter: @troymooney

Facebook: https://www.facebook.com/troymooneyblog/

Website: www.troymooney.com

Herbert O'Neil

Email: Herbert.oneil@lifeschools.net

Twitter: @herbertoneiljr

Website: www.herbertoneil.com

Dedicated to

Coach Garlen "Wade" McLain

1956-2011

Believer, Husband, Father, Educator, Coach

To me a Faithful Friend-TM

Estella Robinson O'Neil

1952-2015

My Beautiful Mother

My First Love -HO

Acknowledgements

Thank you to the following who formally or informally helped us with suggestions throughout the writing process: Courtney Carpenter, Eddie Coulson, Angie Davis, Kristen Hebert, Kirsten Hund, Tam Jones, Brandon Palmer, Richard Valenta, Lorrie Welch.

Contents

Preface

I want you to succeed in your new position as principal. The principalship is the most difficult job in education. There is a shortage of quality principals and the students in your community need you to be successful to improve their own chances of success. Joining a new campus, even in a familiar district, requires you to develop an entrance strategy. A strategy for you to avoid the mistakes that can irreparably damage your leadership effectiveness and that encourages you to wait to make changes until you have connected with your stakeholders.

This handbook and subsequent revisions represent my effort at sharing the best practices acquired through experience, relationships, mentoring, and research. The ideas are heavily influenced from countless conversations with the great people I have been able to work with at Waller ISD, Fort Bend ISD, Life Schools of Dallas, social media, and throughout my career.

I have worked in a traditional public school district, a public charter, and served on the board of a private school. I have also observed or assisted schools in many states and three foreign countries (Brazil, India, and Honduras). Those experiences have confirmed for me that while there are many different education models that can meet the needs of a student and their family, all of the models require effective campus leaders. Becoming an effective campus leader starts with a successful entry into the new position.

I am forever indebted to my mentor Danny Twardowski, current superintendent of the Waller Independent School District in Texas. Beyond hiring me for four different jobs over my career, he has provided an incredible example of a great principal who meets the needs of those they lead and serve. There are few like him.

Additionally, I would like to thank many others who have assisted me in my professional growth. Gregg Matte, Herbert O'Neil, Kelly Baehren, Joe Graham, Wade McLain, Jim Phillips, Mike Miller, Richard McReavy, Jonathan Lowden, Brian Merrell, Angie Davis, Michael McKie, Mark Foust, Kevin Moran, Michael Twigg, Lincoln Goodwin, Brent Wilson, Barry West, Charles

Pulliam, Jennifer Wilson, Scott Fuller, Bryant DeBord and the countless other dear friends who have shaped my character and increased my understanding of leadership.

Troy Mooney

My best times in education were when I served as a campus principal. It is the toughest, yet most rewarding job in education. I was fortunate enough to serve as a new principal for three campuses, and to jump in at a fourth spot. I learned many things at each spot, and I certainly would have loved to have a guide to help me through it all.

I have been blessed to work in three wonderful districts. I still have many friends in Waller ISD where I started as a teacher/coach and an assistant principal. It was in Corsicana ISD where I learned the true ropes. Serving as the principal of Drane Intermediate, Collins Middle School, and Corsicana High School were days filled with joy as well as multiple challenges. I am thankful for all of those experiences.

I am always thankful for my mentor and friend, Troy Mooney who took a chance on a young man from Hearne, TX to teach English to 7th graders. I have always been able to call and get sound advice when I simply had no clue of what I was doing.

Herbert O'Neil

Introduction

Knowledge, skills, personal characteristics, values, and beliefs are all factors that contribute to the success of a principal and improved student outcomes. Without a good entry plan, however, the principal will never have a chance to leverage their strengths in those areas. A poor entry into their new position will diminish their chances of success. A few early, bad decisions can irreparably damage even the most promising new leader.

You can likely recall memories of principals who made poor decisions at the start of their new assignments. For me I think of three examples. One principal alienated their new staff at the first meeting by declaring that the campus was broken, another created immediate rebellion by detailing numerous changes in their first ever staff email (before meeting the staff), while a third attempted to replicate all of the systems that worked at their previous campus without learning first about their new one. Each of these well intentioned new principals started their job with a poor entry plan. The following sections of this book list out the many components of a successful entry plan. Jump around to whichever area you think you should study first, but remember the foundation of your principalship is rooted in your relationships.

Hugs, Handshakes and High Fives

Herbert O'Neil penned this blog post about the importance of relationships for any principal but especially a new one. It is a good reminder to you of what is most important.

-TM

I still remember my first principal job. I remember one of our teachers telling me later in my first year that she thought I would be a push over because I had a big smile on my face in the press release that was in the paper. It didn't help either that I was a young fella. One thing that I enjoyed as a teacher and an assistant principal was that I always had pretty good student-teacher and administrator relationships. I figured out early on that if they knew you cared, they would never let you down. I struggled, though, early on because I wanted the students to behave well. The previous principal did a great job with them, and I didn't want to lose that.

One thing I had to realize was that I had to be Herbert. I simply couldn't be anyone else. I wanted to enjoy the students, and I wanted them to enjoy the school. So I woke up one morning and decided that I wouldn't let anything get in the way of having great relationships with our students.

It hit me! Everyday had to be a day of hugs, handshakes, and high fives! Why? Because kids need it! You do not know what they are bringing into the school, and as the school leader you have the ability to brighten their day each day. I challenge every principal to greet their students with either a hug, handshake, or a high five each day. My students learned quickly that I would show love, have fun, and cut up with them every day. With that in mind all students had to live up to the expectations that we set for them, and I meant it. They knew I didn't play. Their education was far too important.

At every level, intermediate, middle and high school I continued to give hugs, handshakes, and high fives. It worked for me, and I never allowed the effective operational management of the campus to suffer. It was quite okay that some of them liked their principal. By the way, it made for a much better day!

So whatever it is: a hug, a handshake, or a high-five, find what works for that particular student. Get to know their names, and have fun with them. You have a tough job; you might as well have fun with the students while you do it.

The First Time Meeting the Staff

The first time I met my staff at Kempner High School was at the end of the day on the last staff work day before summer vacation. That was not the time for me to lay out my "21 points of light" to these exhausted educators who were ready to meet the new guy and start their summer vacation.

　-TM

I always had large amounts of anxiety when I met my staff for the first time. I always knew that it didn't need to be a long meeting and I needed to brag on them about something great that had occurred in the previous school year. I always felt that they mostly wanted to know that they mattered to me.

　-HO

T he first time you meet your staff is the best opportunity to make a good impression (profound wisdom right?). The staff will primarily be concerned with how you and your plans and leadership practices will personally impact them. The staff will have researched you on social media, former campus websites, and through conversations with their professional networks. This first meeting is not the time to unveil any new changes. Any new change will be rightfully perceived as autocratic rather than collaboratively developed. This first meeting is more about communicating your eagerness to get to know and work alongside the staff and less about sharing your personal accomplishments and new plans for the campus. You should have learned about some recent successes of the campus prior to this meeting and then share them with the staff. You should reveal that you are aware the campus staff has already been doing great things prior to your selection for this position. Your supervisor, or the previous principal may control planning the time and date of the introductory meeting with the faculty. Be flexible. If 3:00 the day before summer vacation worked for me, then you can make anytime work.

Checklist of what should be communicated at the first meeting:

- Positive, recent accomplishments of the campus and the staff.

- A desire to work alongside the staff

- If possible, something positive about previous leadership

- An interest in building professional relationships with the staff and a reference to any current efforts underway to begin that process

- The desirability and appeal of the position of principal of this campus.

The message should be brief and then you should linger to interact with the staff. Sharing generic positive goals is acceptable, but avoid specifics as this creates change related stress.

Checklist of what should not be communicated at the first meeting:

I have already shared the story about the principal who, at their first meeting with the staff, announced that the school was in a state of emergency. The fact is the school probably was in a state of

emergency, but the first meeting was not the time to say that. The

principal was gone by the end of the year.

     -TM

- Any intended changes unless there is a critical safety or
security issue
- Specific goals
- Any statements that convey that you think the new campus is
in a state of crisis or emergency
- Any statements that convey that you are arriving with all of
the answers to fix any problems.
- Lengthy list of your personal accomplishments (not sure this
should ever be something you share, let the praise come from
someone else)

The Listening Tour

My friend Gregg Matte once shared with me how important it is for people to feel fully known and fully loved in their important relationships. Similarly, as the principal you have to eliminate any feelings of anonymity from your staff by conveying that you are aware of them and understand their contributions

    -TM

T he quote attributed to G. K. Chesterton," Never tear down a fence until you determine why it was built." is a good reminder for you in your new position. Listening, observing, and building relationships before instituting changes is your best approach. Listening intently to understand the needs of the staff, students, and community is known as a *Listening Tour*. The listening tour provides you the necessary time and effort to discover necessary changes and to reveal any potential unintended

consequences of those changes. The listening tour is also the first

step towards building necessary relationships. Everyone on the staff

wants to perceive that they have a special relationship with you.

They need affirmation that you know them personally and that you

know how they contribute to campus success. It is your

responsibility to attempt to meet individually with all of the staff.

These meetings involve listening to concerns and ideas, learning

about the employee personally, and discovering how they understand

their contribution to the campus. Take notes when you meet with

your staff and restate their ideas back to them to confirm that you

have received their message.

Meeting the former principal

At Kempner High School, we instituted a special day once a year (K

DAY) where we brought back the former principals and teachers of

the year for an annual luncheon. This tradition persists today at that

campus. It is a great way to honor the contributions of previous leadership and staff.

    -TM

When I was principal of Collins Middle School, one of the former

principals had served as principal over 25 years. He lived around

the corner from the school and had not returned since he retired 10

years prior. The staff loved him! We named the library in his honor,

and invited him back for all school faculty lunches. They loved

seeing Mr. Hall in the building. I was made better because of his

presence.

    -HO

Unless there is a compelling reason to not do so, you should meet

with the previous principal. The former principal can provide

general insight into key decisions made the previous year or

specifics about items such as the campus master schedule. The

former principal can also give updates on current campus initiatives

and unresolved problems. If possible, the former principal should be

praised publicly and thanked for their contributions during their

tenure at an early staff meeting. Remember that many of your staff will be in regular communication with the former principal through sharing updates on how things are going under your leadership. If you ever find yourself in the position of being a former principal, avoid disparaging the new leader. After all you left the campus and probably are in no position to help anyone that remains other than by encouraging them to work with their new leader to resolve problems and concerns.

Meeting other applicants

In both of my jobs as a principal, current assistants had also applied for the position. It is a credit to their character on how well they handled that situation. Rather than feel threatened, consider they might be an asset to your tenure as the campus principal.

-TM

You should meet with all other current campus employees who applied for the principal position. These other applicants are most likely high performers. The will still have influence on the campus and the community. Some of them may have been the favored candidates of the former principal, a school board member, or someone else in the district leadership. Meeting with these other applicants provides you a chance to assess their current attitudes and feelings, and their desire to continue working at the campus.

Meeting other principals in the district

When I joined Fort Bend ISD, I scheduled visits with most of the other ten high school principals within two weeks of my first day. I formed invaluable relationships and thankfully created some decent first impressions that were then shared throughout the district. These visits smoothed pathways and created connections for me around the district and at my own campus. I discovered that two of the principals had been teachers on my campus earlier in their careers and still had numerous staff connections on my staff.

-TM

As soon as I started service as principal in Corsicana ISD I couldn't wait to meet the other principals that I would be working with.

Corsicana was a special community with a rich history, and the principals that had been there for many years knew much more about it than I did. They taught me the ropes and helped me through things that I would have struggled with without their guidance.

-HO

Meet with as many of the other principals at your same level in the district as possible. In a larger district this may be limited to nearby principals, or members of your feeder pattern only. In a smaller district meet with principals at any level or even neighboring district principals. Failing to meet with them will result in these other principals developing opinions of you from other sources. The difficulties of the principalship require a support network with other principals that is best developed before any crisis. These other principals may have worked in the district for many years, worked at your campus previously, or live in your campus attendance zone. They will have many connection points with your campus. After you meet with them, these other principals can help you build support at your own campus.

Meeting with the Administrative Assistant

My first administrative assistant in Corsicana was married to a local celebrity. Her husband served as Head Football Coach of many winning Corsicana Tiger Football teams, as well as the Head Football Coach at Texas A&M University at one time. She knew everyone in town and was well respected in all circles. She was the lifeblood of the campus, and everyone knew it. She was a great asset to me as I transitioned into the principalship, and helped me understand the unique dynamics of our historic campus.

  -HO

The administrative assistant is one of the most critical relationships for any principal. Failing to establish a regular routine to meet and exchange information with the administrative assistant will marginalize the principal. At the first meeting, it is important to learn from the administrative assistant about effective procedures they have used in the past. The new principal needs to learn the "heart" of their administrative assistant and how they think they

26

contribute to campus success. Most administrative assistants are informal leaders on the campus. Failure to nurture this crucial relationship will create discontent with some of the staff. Sharing calendaring and email passwords and responsibilities with the administrative assistant will free up time for important rather than urgent tasks. The new principal needs to obtain an emergency contact list from the administrative assistant and have the assistant add important dates to the calendar including, for example, all of the staff birthdays and special recognition weeks. The new principal will quickly need to schedule regular meetings with the administrative assistant.

Meeting other campus staff

At my second principal position, I asked that my administrative assistant invite all of my staff to meet with me individually during the summer. The meetings were short 15-30 minute conversations but they were invaluable to us having a good start to the school year.

    -TM

The people that I had the best relationships with were the individuals

that I had the pleasure of meeting with before the school year

started. As a new principal having the opportunity to meet with your

staff individually is second to none. I would learn about their family,

favorite restaurants in town, and their hope for the future of the

school. You don't want to miss doing this!

   -HO

Meet with the associate and assistant principals, team leaders,

counselors, registrar, campus athletic coordinator, lead facilities and

food service employees, and any other managers or leaders on the

campus. There should also be a formal communication with all of

the staff about your desire and availability to meet. Not everyone

will want to meet with you, but those who do will have agendas they

want to share that you need to hear. Those who decide to meet with

you will give you insight into the informal leadership networks on

the campus. The most critical reason to offer to meet with everyone

is because it is the best way to start building relationships.

Meeting special programs leaders

Meet with the Special Education, English Language Learner, Dyslexia, Gifted and Talented, and other special programs leaders to understand any immediate support, supply, or scheduling needs for those areas. Quickly scheduling meetings with these leaders conveys the appropriate sense of interest in these important programs. For many of these leaders you might be the first principal to take a sincere interest in their programs.

Meeting students

Is there anything better than meeting the students? They are the reason we entered into this profession. Some of my best moments the summer before starting my time as a high school principal were early mornings at cross country practice, seeing the cheerleaders off to camp, attending two a day football practices and a leadership luncheon with all of the club presidents.

-TM

Meeting my students was my most favorite part of the job. What's funny is that I would be so nervous. Of course I wanted them to respect me, but I always wanted them to know that I cared about them and that I was always working on their behalf. Take time to attend their extracurricular events early on if you work at a high school. If the students do not have extracurricular events meet them where they are...On the playground, in the cafeteria, and before and after school.

-HO

You can quickly build relationships with secondary students by meeting with student leaders. These include members of student government, club presidents, and extracurricular officers. Hosting luncheons, scheduling personal meetings, or attending any extracurricular events are good summer activities to begin building those necessary relationships. At the elementary and junior high levels there are fewer opportunities to informally meet the students before school begins, but be creative to find ways to connect to club and activity leaders.

Meeting other district staff

As a new principal in a new district I always wanted to meet the transportation director very quickly. Why? There was always something going on with transportation. Many of our students arrive to school by school bus, and anytime you take a trip it impacts transportation. Having a good relationship with the transportation director is crucial to your success as a principal. There are many other key players throughout the district that you need to set up meetings with and go visit. The more people that can help and support you during your first year the better.

    -HO

Depending on the size of the school system there will be other directors and managers to meet with and it will help you out to meet these staff prior to any crisis situation. You will want to have made contact prior to making a call about loss of power or water, an issue with a school bus, or a lack of food in the cafeteria at lunchtime.

These other managers include district leaders for transportation, maintenance, food service, athletics, and fine arts. Meeting with these leaders begins the relationship building process and reveals to you how those leaders view their current operational interactions with the campus. Ask them to come visit your campus and show you what they need from you to do their own jobs successfully.

Meeting other stakeholders

A first meeting I had with a stakeholder was over whether or not I would support their request to change the Project Graduation location from an offsite venue to the campus. While this event had not been on my checklist, I quickly realized that this decision impacted my seniors, my PTO, fundraising efforts, and many campus club sponsors.

-TM

Parent Teacher Organization Officers, parent volunteers, local civic and community leaders, and leaders of organizations that regularly rent out the campus facility are just a few suggestions of necessary first meetings with other stakeholders. These other stakeholders likely will be concerned about you changing some successful arrangement they had with the previous principal. They will have influence in the community. Find a way to meet with them to understand what they need to be successful and whether or not you will be able to continue accommodating their requests.

Exploring the Physical Plant

Q uickly explore the physical plant of the campus. Explore initially as part of a guided tour and then separately on your own to confirm you have all necessary keys, access cards, codes, and combinations. Discover all entrances, exits, and other special interior locations. Open doors to all closets and storage areas during the physical plant examination. This prevents future surprise discoveries. Learn how to use the public address, bell, and alarm system operations and then create reference cards or notes for those devices. Collect the contact numbers for all emergency maintenance providers and review the district procedures for contacting those providers during a crisis. Learn how to operate the microphone system for assemblies (and go ahead and order some replacement microphones as you can never have enough.) Spend time with the campus facility staff to learn any special or frequently troublesome features of the building.

Learning the Master Schedule

T he master schedule should be reviewed with anyone who helped to create the schedule. Ask questions about staff assignments, projected class sizes, room locations, floating teachers, class times, and lunch to understand the reasons behind the scheduling decisions. Determine if any staff have additional conference, duty, or planning periods. Find out if the campus has common planning or professional learning community time built into the schedule. Review the schedule with the administrative team, counselors, team leaders, special programs staff, and electives coordinators. This ensures everyone is aware of scheduling assignments. Review the schedule to determine if there is time for intervention during the day. A year of observing and learning is a good practice before making any master schedule changes.

Developing a Shared Vision

The importance of shared vision

Without a vision there is no clarity concerning what you trying to accomplish. There is little incentive for employees to give you their "discretionary effort" without understanding and then agreeing with the campus vision. A shared vision increases employee energy and engagement, and creates meaning and purpose for employees. A vision provides a mental image for the future ideal state of the school and orients everyone towards reaching that goal. A vision stimulates imagination and attracts commitment from stakeholders.

Understanding the current state of the campus

Your various meetings with staff, listening and observing, and your visibility and accessibility, all combine to create the necessary environment for developing a shared vision. You must nurture relationships and allow the stakeholders to engage in individual and collective discovery learning as part of the vision development process. The first step for developing a shared vision is to understand the school as it currently exists

Sharing and modeling values and beliefs

Sharing and modeling consistent values and beliefs with the staff is another important early step in the process of developing a shared vision. What you do is more powerful than what you say you believe. Your work ethic, where you spend your time during the day, demeanor, and interactions and rapport with staff and students all provide evidence of your values and beliefs. Slogans and rallying cries are important to sharing values and beliefs, but your actions are what crystallizes those values and beliefs for the staff and students.

What is the mission?

The mission explains why the campus exists, reveals why the campus does what it does, and states what is important and what will be accomplished. Clarifying the mission reminds people about what their purpose is at the campus. The mission defines the purpose. Everyone working in the school should believe that improving student outcomes is their purpose regardless of their job function. Emphasizing purpose over function will help the school system organize around what it is trying to accomplish (the mission) rather than what is being done (activities). The mission of Primer, for example, is to prepare and support school leaders who can transform schools and improve outcomes for all students. As a new principal, you will need to lead a collaborative mission development activity for your campus no later than the end of your first year.

What is the vision?

40

The vision reveals the desired state of the campus. The vision is where the organization wants to go and what it plans to become. Employees who embrace the vision are more likely to be fully engaged and to give discretionary effort. Employees who understand the vision are able to see how their own work matters for the campus. The vision is inspirational. The vision is what is possible if everyone aligns their efforts. Almost any principal, even ineffective principals with poor entry plans, will have no problem creating the vision for their campus. Most leaders know what they want to see or want to happen. The difficult part, though, is developing a shared vision that everyone understands and adopts. A successful entry plan makes it easier to develop a shared vision.

New principal efforts to develop a mission and vision

Prior to engaging in any mission or vision development activities with the staff, you should complete your early meetings with all stakeholders to begin understanding the campus. A mission or vision

41

that is created and shared without first building relationships and then listening to concerns will be viewed as the sole creation of the principal. Mission and vision statements that endure, engage, and inspire employees are collaboratively developed.

What is your rallying cry?

At one campus my rallying cry was the Home of Champions. Every day I would remind the kids that they attended the Home of Champions. When I would read off their accomplishments on the public address I would end my message by saying, "we are the home of champions." I have been told by more than one staff member that it got "corny" after a while, but I never relented in reminding the students how I felt about them.

    -TM

You Belong Here

We are a relevant, systematic, community

We are the Home of Champions

Purpose, Passion, Pride

Courage, Character, Commitment

Take care of the Three As-Academics, Attendance, Attitude

The above are examples of school leader rallying cries. Find a way to encapsulate some of your core beliefs into a group of three words or a short slogan. This will keep your beliefs and values at top of mind awareness for your staff or for your students. Use your rallying cry when you speak on the public address system, in your email signature, on your meeting agendas, and on signage.

Make Your Meetings Matter

It is your responsibility as a leader to make sure your meetings

matter. You cannot delegate this responsibility.

   -TM

O ne of the first ways you will be judged as a leader is in your ability to lead a meeting through an agenda and to keep participants focused on the key agenda issues. The starting point for effectively leading a meeting is to only have essential meetings. Meetings can be essential to you or essential to the other attendees or both. The following guidelines are for your formal meetings with faculty leaders, administrative team, campus site based decision making team or other similar teams. There are other formats to use for stand up or check-ins or other less formal meetings. Before any meeting, even pre-scheduled meetings, always determine if it is necessary to actually meet.

Before the meeting

If the meeting passes the "essentialness test" then these are the
questions to answer before the meeting:

- What are the products? *If there are no products (or action
  items) then consider cancelling the meeting.*
- Who needs to attend?
- Where will you meet? *Resolve all scheduling, presentation,
  and room set-up issues before the meeting*

Developing the agenda for the meeting

The agenda is the contract for the meeting between you and the
participants about what will be discussed and produced at the
meeting. It is a reference point to refocus the participants if they

become sidetracked with other discussions.

For recurring meetings, always review the most prior agenda and the agenda from the previous year for that same meeting. The reasons for reviewing the previous year's agenda are to remind you of the things you were concerned about at this same time during the previous year. In the cyclical school business those same issues, deadlines, or concerns tend to reappear annually.

Solicit your attendees for agenda item topics prior to the meeting. This accomplishes two goals. First it alerts you to the areas of concern of the participants prior to the meeting. Second, it eliminates the practice of offering surprise topics during meetings. These surprise topics can quickly derail a meeting. Since you have asked for topics ahead of time, you can remind anyone that presents a surprise topic that the topic can be discussed at the next meeting. Every once in a while you may want to discuss a surprise topic, but by soliciting beforehand you establish a ready professional response to any unwanted discussion.

Present your agenda in draft form to attendees before the meeting so that they can both prepare for the meeting and confirm if any of their own agenda submissions were included. You do not want the attendees arriving unprepared to make critical decisions and plans for the campus.

Leading the meeting

Start on time. Even if being on time is not important to you it is at least important to some of your team. Starting meetings late communicates to everyone who was punctual that their time is not valuable to you. Starting late also conveys that you are unprepared. Your staff will quickly adjust to the "real" start time and soon will be arriving when they guess you will start the meeting.

Keep the meeting focused on the agenda. If you have presenters, find out what they are going to share and establish your expectations for the length of their presentation. The agenda should cover all of the critical information and decisions for this meeting. Refocus the meeting when you feel you are no longer progressing through the agenda.

Throughout the meeting keep track of newly developed action items by maintaining a "who does what for whom by when" list. Keeping record of action items quickly resolves the "we should do something about this issue" statements that are offered up in meetings. At the end of the meeting, each participant should restate to you any action items assigned to them to confirm they understand what they are to do and when they are to do it.

After the meeting

Summarize any important decisions or action items in a follow-up email, save your agenda to help you prepare for the next meeting (and next year's meeting!), and keep track of the list of attendees.

Further ways to improve your meetings

- **Choose different meeting formats**

Meeting in different locations, having stand-up check-ins, and making changes to the seating arrangements can create different formats for your meetings. Experiment with the best format for the products and participants for each meeting.

- **Allow time for collaborative problem solving**

Allow time in the meeting to step back and let the participants work through solutions to agenda topics. Just because you are leading the meeting does not mean you need to be doing all the talking. Small group formats that report to the whole group either through a quick presentation or through a shared online document work best to quickly generate and then disseminate solutions.

- **Get comfortable with saying "I don't know"**

If during a meeting you are pressed to make a decision for which you are unprepared, simply say "I don't know" and then announce an action item to revisit the issue either with a smaller group or at a future meeting.

- **Include professional growth and continuous learning in all of your meetings**

Share a video or book summary, lead a problem based learning discussion, or ask for a report from attendees of recent professional development. Find a way to grow your teams at each of your meetings. All of your key players want to grow.

- **Make the meeting comfortable**

Provide snacks or lunch, adjust room temperature, create good seating arrangements, and play music at the start to make the meeting comfortable for attendees

Other Key Actions for a New Principal

My first principal supervisor told me that in year one I should keep him informed of everything I was doing for the first time.

 -TM

T here is no end to the list of key actions for a new principal. Every action you take is a key action. Every time you answer a question you are creating new campus procedures. What follows in this section are a few of the many "other" key actions for a new principal.

Communicating with supervisors

Most supervisors do not want to be surprised. Assume your supervisors are like most supervisors and keep them informed of your actions and concerns. It is a good idea to get clarity on which decisions your supervisor wants to only be informed about and which ones they want to have more involvement with during your early tenure as a new principal.

Championing your culture

This blog post from Herbert O'Neil is from the end of a school year, but serves as a good reminder for new principals to begin championing their culture throughout the year.

-TM

Let's be honest, April is a tough time in the life of a school. There are so many things going on and it seems like the finish line can't come fast enough. I still remember the days when I served as a principal just trying to cross the finish line with everything deleted off my never ending list.

I have talked to several principal and assistant principal friends over the last couple of weeks and have found that the message is constant for all of them. They feel tired and over worked and are locked in a completely thankless job. When I hear them speak I think of what I often call the dark days of the principalship. I hear the stories of taking donuts and juice to cheer folks up only to hear "Well, why didn't the principal bring breakfast tacos?" Or to surprise folks with Whataburger gift cards only to hear "I don't eat hamburgers, they should have gotten a variety for us." Yeah, these things do happen. I also hear from campus leaders who speak of the never ending mandates that may or may not come from Central Office. It gets tough!

Principals and assistant principals I want to remind you even in the midst of a million and one things going on, to never forget to Champion Your Culture. I believe that the culture of your school is the responsibility of all in the building. Everyone must work together to make it a great learning and extracurricular space for students. The tough thing is that many forget that while they are busy with the day to day of the school. So here are a few tips to help you Champion Your Culture during April:

- Don't forget your vision for the school. Everyone was fired up about it at the first staff meeting after summer break. Remind them about it over the PA, in department/team meetings, and in all correspondence to staff, students, and parents.

- Find positive spaces at the campus and highlight them. Go to the areas of your campus that are beaming with positivity and talk about it over the PA, in department/team meetings, and in all correspondence to staff, students, and parents.

- Surprise your staff with meaningful small celebrations. Go to their room and celebrate them about something you saw them do well that aligns with the school vision in front of their students. Sometimes this is much better and more sustainable than those fattening donuts you spent money on.

- Be super visible! In front of the school, before school, in the cafeteria, and in the hallways constantly. I know you have meetings, and that's ok...Move them around so people can see your smiling face.

- Folks who have a Negative Nancy complex should be told they are negative to their face. Yes, this can be controversial. But if you want to Champion Your Culture you have to let them know. Be professional, be kind, but be serious. Let them know you do not appreciate it.

- Spend time with students. Go into classrooms with them. Sit and shoot the breeze with them at lunch. Go to their events. If the students celebrate the work of the school and how the leader supports them, it will cascade through the school.

- Exercise tough love with your students. Our precious students become more excited when Spring is in the air. Having a lack of discipline on your campus can wreck your culture. Love the students, but ensure that all student behavior issues are taken care of. Discipline issues need to be taken care of quickly with follow up to the teacher.

- Don't forget to have fun! The entire school community should see you having fun. If you look tired and beat down, then the school will look tired and beat down. So have fun!

This is only a small list of things you can do to ensure that you Champion Your Culture. There are many other things that can be listed to improve school culture during the tough times. Being a campus administrator is a great job filled with unique challenges but with the right care many lives can be changed.

Concern - Genuine concern for others

Early in my career as an assistant principal, my mentor told me that I was moving around too fast and only focusing on crossing tasks off my to-do list rather than investing in the people I was serving. I have always been more comfortable completing tasks than strengthening relationships, and you may be that way also, but you must commit to maintaining your connections with others or you will fail as a principal.

-TM

The principals that succeed long term are those who are intentional about nurturing staff and student relationships. It is quickly apparent to others if the principal is concerned about others or solely focused on their own career advancement. People want to work for leaders who are mindful of their employee's best interests and genuinely care for them. I heard a speaker from a service academy share that while employees want leaders who are always learning and who can make tough decisions, they most want leaders who are genuinely concerned for them as a person.

Decision Making - Making difficult decisions

This advice comes from a former superintendent named Gordon Anderson who shared these thoughts in a memo with my mentor in 1993 before he entered into his first principal role.

   -TM

Every decision you will make involves risk and your personal judgment. Usually they are a consideration of alternatives and rarely a simple choice between good and bad. Decisions often take time to mature before you see the results of your choice. Test your decisions by seeking advice and perspective of others. Every major decision is like surgery; it is an intervention into a system that carries with it the risk of shock. Many effective decisions are distasteful.

Your decisions must be appropriate for the capacity of the people

who have the responsibility for implementation. You will learn some

of your most important lessons from your bad decisions.

Delegate - Delegating Properly

*Ask the people with the best ability to solve problems to solve those
problems*

　　-TM

You will quickly find yourself doing all kinds of urgent work as a

new principal. A sustainable practice is to figure out what only the

principal can do and then delegate the rest to your staff and

administrative team. Even in a small school you will need to create

a plan to train certain staff to resolve issues that do not need to be

directly handled by the principal. Delegating is an effective way to

continually share with the staff what is important to you and what

you are trying to accomplish as a leader. Some leaders tend to avoid delegating because they ultimately do not trust others to carry out the tasks or complete the work to the same degree of excellence. That could be true for your organization. However, the solution is not to avoid delegating but rather to grow and develop your team. Another problem with not delegating is you do not allow those working with you to participate and invest themselves in the work. High performers will not stay long in an environment where they are not making a contribution. Never delegate the same job to two different people without designating a project lead, and always be clear about what kinds of interval reporting you want on your project (if any).

Demeanor - Welcoming demeanor

The principal receives a steady dose of bad news nearly every day they are on the job. It is the nature of leadership. People want to unload their burdens onto the leader.

 -TM

The expression on the principal's face sets the tone for the staff. You should train yourself to not overreact to bad news. Whenever you are working through difficult conversations or solving crisis events be mindful of the non-verbal cues your facial expressions are sending to the staff. The staff looks to the leader for an indication if things are going well or if things are going poorly. The face of the principal "says it all" about the state of the campus. Principals are nearly always busy, but it is important to not appear rushed, harried, or overworked. Employees like to know that their principal works hard, but a principal who appears to be always in a hurry is conveying that they do not have time to meet with their staff. Your ability to discern which tasks only the principal can do and to delegate effectively (and develop staff to accomplish those items) will impact your ability to provide necessary time for your staff.

Expectations - Establishing expectations

Sometimes we want to avoid having a difficult conversation in hopes the issue will just resolve itself. How often does that really work? In fact, if you fail to share your expectations early or to address behavior outside of those expectations at an early stage then you will

actually be training your staff to behave contradictory to what you

really want.

-TM

Rather than what is said, it is what is done by the new principal and

tolerated in their presence that will establish the expectations for the

staff. It is better to address things that fall outside of expectations

earlier than later. As a new principal, after your initial first

meetings, quickly establish and clarify expectations with your

administrative team and staff. Understanding those expectations

helps the staff to comfortably adjust to your new leadership. There

are ways to do this better than just giving an expectations list to

people. Instead, model what you expect while also having one-on-

one meetings with your administrative team to help them understand

what you want them to do and how you want them to do it.

Learn - Commit to continuously learn

Dr. Joe Graham (@RealJoeGraham) was my first colleague mentor as a new principal. Joe was a principal in a nearby district. He and I would meet face-to-face once a year for dinner and also communicate throughout the year to share our ideas, things we had learned, and plans for our own campuses. The professional growth I experienced during those times helped me tremendously during those early years as a principal.

     -TM

The principalship is overwhelming, especially during the first year. However, you need to commit to continuously learning. Utilize social media personal learning networks, attend a conference, read books, find a mentor colleague or some other method to ensure that you are staying relevant and growing professionally. The overflow of your own learning (or shared learning) will become the content you will share with staff and students and it will help you better develop the other members of your administrative team.

The first book I would recommend for any new principal is *First Break All the Rules* by Marcus Buckingham and Curt Coffman.

Perspective - Look beyond your perspective

It seemed empowering for me to return to my staff and criticize a central office decision by saying "I don't know what they are thinking", or "They don't know what they are doing." But in reality all I was doing is revealing to my staff that I lacked the influence or involvement to get what I needed for the campus. Rather than criticize, I should have chosen to learn the why behind decisions at an earlier stage of my principalship.

-TM

At every level including your new role as a principal you are exposed to a new perspective. Be aware that your campus perspective is not the same as your supervisor's perspective who will have a larger view of a feeder pattern, or the entire district. Keep that in mind as you react to decisions such as a denial of your request for a staff member or additional supplies. The best thing you can do for your campus, your career, and your supervisor, is to stretch your understanding to observe and learn a broader perspective. Don't see issues only through the lens of how they affect your campus, but rather attempt to understand how the events all fit together throughout the district (or even at the state or national level). Adopting this perspective will eliminate you embracing a victim mentality and better equip you to explain events to your own staff and students.

Response - Responding to requests for changing practice or procedure early in your tenure

During the first few weeks of the school year of both of my tenures as a new campus principal, I was approached by staff with requests to make changes to existing practice or procedure at the campus. Sometimes the requests seemed so simple or beneficial that I was tempted to make a quick affirmative decision. A quick decision would show that I was a decisive leader. It also would have been disastrous in most cases.

    -TM

While you may want to demonstrate your quick intellect when approached with requests to make changes, a better response is to ask the petitioner, "What have we done before and why did it not work." Based on their response you will know who all would be impacted by your off the cuff decision, who you should then meet with prior to making a decision, and why the staff member thinks things are not working well at the current time.

Routine - Embrace routine and structure

Your students and staff want to feel safe and secure while they are at work or school. Routines and structure increase feelings of safety and security, alleviate stress, and create better environments for improving student outcomes. The cyclical nature of the school business lends itself to establishing routines for annual or daily events. Complex events such as graduations, pep rallies, or the start of school, are much smoother when everyone knows what to expect. Embracing routine does not mean abandoning innovation, rather it is an acknowledgement that a school is basically a small city and works better when things are planned rather than haphazardly implemented.

Survey - Surveying the staff

I recommend waiting until the previous principal has vacated the building before conducting any surveys. I did not wait one time and it was something the previous principal told me he thought I should have done after the fact. Looking back, I can see how that would have made him uncomfortable as it would have made me uncomfortable had our roles been reversed.

   -TM

Conduct an initial staff survey such as the "Start-Keep-Stop" (SKS) survey to develop a beginning needs assessment of the campus. A sample of the SKS survey is included in the appendices to this handbook. The survey of any campus is just one data point and should be viewed in conjunction with information gathered from the individual staff meetings and observation. In my history of reviewing surveys from my own campuses and for other campuses, certain problems are highly likely to appear during any principal transition such as dress code enforcement for students and/or staff, student tardiness, and discipline response and consequences. My surveys were always by default anonymous, but I had the option for employees to sign their name if they wanted to speak to me directly about the issue. Surveying the staff is a good practice throughout your tenure. You need multiple feedback mechanisms to make sure what you think is happening on the campus is a shared perception of your staff.

Visibility - Be visible or be misunderstood

When you accept the role of principal, you are also committing to spend a lot of time watching other people's children perform at athletic, fine arts, and academic competitions. You will not be successful if you are not visible at these events and available to your parents and students in those less formal settings. You do not have to stay the whole time but make sure people see you cheering on their children, or enjoying their performances. If you are not visible in this manner, then you will be misunderstood. Your absence will be interpreted as a lack of commitment to the school. Without a chance to easily speak to you for clarifications, your decisions will be misinterpreted and then criticized. Your lack of presence will result in people saying you do not listen to their concerns. Most importantly, whenever you are dealing with challenges and crises, you will not have the parents and the students giving you the benefit of the doubt because they will not have a relationship with you.

Thriving in the Lonely World of the Principalship

It is lonely being a principal.

> *-TM*

The stakeholders of the school view you as the ultimate position of authority and leadership in the school. Though in constant contact with others all day, you will feel lonely and should expect many existing relationships to change as a result of your new role. People approach you with needs to be met more often than just for casual conversation. You will have more superficial but fewer deeper relationships, at least early in your tenure, with your campus staff. Developing relationships with other principals, choosing a mentor, and participating in professional organizations and activities are some of the ways in which you can maintain meaningful professional relationships. Of all of these activities the most important for you is to find a good mentor to help you through difficult decisions.

Conclusion

T his book contains many recommended suggestions for you as a new principal. These suggestions describe our personal pathways to successful entry, if you follow them you will likely succeed. A final reminder is to always thoughtfully consider your actions and decisions. Unless it is an issue of safety, most decisions do not need to be made immediately. You will regret the unintended consequences of most of your hasty decisions. "Go slow to go fast." Go slow first and build the necessary relationships that will enable you to go fast later.

Good luck in your quest to become the principal your students and staff desperately need,

Troy Mooney

Herbert O'Neil

Appendices

Appendix A

Summer Activities Checklist for

Principals

Building Readiness

- Monitoring of summer maintenance required repairs

- Room Readiness

    o Fire drill routes

    o Safety kits

    o Required seating

    o Rooms labeled with staff names

    o Supplies

    o Flags

- Hallway and other room signage

Operational and Procedural Readiness

- Master Schedule complete with room assignments

  o Lunch assignments

  o Leveling of classes

- Testing and scheduling of bell system including reviewing modified bell schedules

- Planned meetings scheduled (Completed scheduling of the principal's planned meetings allows others on the staff to then schedule their own meetings). Some suggested meetings to schedule include:

  o Faculty meetings

  o Department Chair/Team Leader meetings

  o Campus horizontal or vertical planning meetings

  o Parent Organization meetings

  o Open House/Meet the Teacher events

  o Site Based Decision Making Team meetings

- Safety Drills scheduled

- Review of function assignments for Administrative teams

  o Responsibilities

  o Duty Assignments

- o Appraisal Assignments
- Select members for any required committees
  - o Attendance Review Committee
  - o Discipline Committee
  - o Campus Improvement Plan Committee
- Duty assignments and duty procedures completed
- Updates made to campus website
  - o Staff changes
  - o Information updates
  - o Calendar update
- Planning for staff return
  - o Key/Computer distribution if applicable
  - o Preparation/Review of required annual forms for staff
    - Handbook acknowledgements
    - Emergency contact updates
    - Parking information
    - Special staff apparel
    - Completion of plan for first week of school that includes the various annual start of school

actions that must be completed by staff and students

- o Prepare meeting agendas for various groups as they return
  - Administrative Team
  - Counselors
  - Department Chairs/Team Leaders
  - New Teachers
  - All Staff
- Planning for student return
  - o Schedule distribution
  - o New student registration
  - o Textbook distribution
  - o Required forms distribution and collection
  - o Identification card distribution
  - o Parking permit distribution
- Review Emergency Operations Plan
- Other campus scheduling
  - o Pep rallies

- o Testing
- Complete plan for required compliance or other annual recommended professional development
  - o Fundraising
  - o Activity account management
  - o Proper relationships/communication with students
  - o Emergency Operations Plan review
  - o Bullying prevention, identification, and response
  - o Campus procedures
  - o Sexual harassment
  - o University Interscholastic League (UIL) training

Staff Communication

- Communication with New Staff
  - o Contact over summer for new teacher professional development requirements
  - o Assigned mentors or "buddies"
- Communication to all staff
  - o Announce any new hires

- Contact over summer for professional development requirements

Student/Parent Communication

- Welcome letter

- Reminder of start of school dates

- Reminder of dress code

Appendix B

Campus Procedures to Learn

Morning Arrival/Drop off

- Bus plan

- Car rider plan

- Walker plan

- Student access plan including staging areas and early morning building access

- Late student arrival procedures

- Student parking plan including parking pass procedures and lot monitoring

Breakfast/Lunch

- Set up and take down procedures for cafeteria seating area preparation

- Cafeteria food service plan including checkout and line

queuing

- Monitoring plan for lines, tables, and cafeteria access hallways

- Seating plan including acceptable alternate eating areas and student movement restrictions during meal times

- Cafeteria cleaning plan between or during lunch service periods

- Applicable cafeteria sound and video equipment operation

Staff procedures

- Sign in/sign out

- Notification of absence

- Preparations for substitutes

- Parking including parking pass procedures

During the day operations

- Building supervision plan

- Tardy procedures

- Administrative two-way radio channel access and charging

procedures.

Maintenance operations

- Building cleaning schedule

- Custodial assigned cleaning areas

Dismissal

- Bus plan

- Car rider plan

- Walker plan

- Plan for students who are not picked up or who do not leave campus at dismissal

- Plan for controlling access after dismissal

- Parking lot monitoring plan

Stakeholder communication

- Public address system operation

- Emergency announcement communication system

- School closing and extracurricular event cancellation

procedures

- Plan for updating stakeholder emergency contacts

Budget procedures

- List of sponsors of campus activity accounts

- Campus activity account guidelines

- Fundraiser approval process

- District budgeting process

Other special procedures:

- Pep rally plan and schedule

- Assembly procedures including student loading and dismissal

  from assembly

Appendix C

Special Event Planning

School events reflect on you. Often these events represent the attendees' only interaction with the school and form the basis for their opinion of the entire campus. A good example of that is a graduation ceremony in which many of the attendees will be visiting the campus or district for the first and only time. The experiences from a well or poorly run event will be shared throughout the community. Most campus special events recur on an annual basis. A good strategy to improve annual campus special events includes the following:

- Detailed recordkeeping of all planning notes, agendas, and copies of other materials from the event.

- Actively soliciting the staff and stakeholders for feedback following the event.

- Updating your planning checklist for the meeting

immediately following the event with any identified modifications or improvements based on observation or feedback

Conducting a Site visit

It is important during the planning process to conduct a site visit of the location of the event. Even if the event is a meeting in an office, visiting the site to review layout, electronics connections, temperature, accessibility, appearance and other data collection activities will help ensure a successful production.

A successful site visit also includes modeling and demonstration of the movement flows of attendees during the event. For example: how will they enter and leave, do they need any signage, is there appropriate queuing area for lines, etc.

Automated Reminders

Utilizing automated annual reminders to begin the planning practice and reviewing notes, materials, and feedback from previous events are other best practices for successful event planning.

Event Project Manager

Designating an Event Project Manager and delegating decision-making authority to that Project Manager is another recommended best practice. Failure to make this designation will lead to decision-making delays and unresolved conflict amongst team members working on the event preparations.

Event Checklist

Utilizing an Event Planning template will minimize the mistakes that characterize poorly planned events. Components of the checklist might include:

Planning for the Event:

- Designate a Project manager
- Select a date for the event (consider setting an inclement weather date)
- Review notes, materials, and feedback from the prior versions of this event (if applicable)
- Establish or review the budget

- Communication with any potential sponsors or vendors

- Reserve event location

- Conduct a Site Walkthrough

- Communicate the event to stakeholders and update all affected calendars

- Event logistics:

  o Security

  o Food and drinks

  o Sound, Photography, and Video

  o Tickets

  o Maintenance and custodial

  o Lighting (inside and for outside parking)

  o Air conditioning/Heating scheduling

  o Signage and directions

  o Parking

  o Agenda for event

  o Scripts for speakers

  o Marketing

  o Invitation list (Board members, Central Office

Administration, etc.)

- o Staff and Volunteer assignments including set up, monitoring and cleanup teams
- o Event supplies

Before the Event

- Confirmation with service providers for the event
- Complete walkthrough
- Sound, Lighting, Video checks
- Temperature check
- Bathroom and other facilities check
- Building access check
- Security check

After the Event

- Solicit feedback from attendees
- Make adjustments to planning notes based on observation and feedback
- Communicate necessary thank-yous

Additional Practices for Certain Special Events

Dances

- Review any proposed themes

- Establish dress code for the dance

- Establish dance attendance eligibility

  - Non-students

  - Parents/Guardians

  - Age restrictions

- Provide rules or guidelines to attendees along with their

  tickets

  - Emphasize pickup time

  - Communicate any dance behavior guidelines

  - Communicate attendance eligibility

- Meet with DJ prior to the event to communicate music

  expectations

Pep Rallies

- Involve everyone affected in the event planning

- Athletics

- Band

- Cheerleading

- Drill Team

- Other as applicable

- Review plans and create contingencies to ensure that the pep rally ends at the correct time rather than too early or too late

- Review and communicate plan for seating in the pep rally location including student entrance and exit from the pep rally

Appendix D

The SKS Survey

Overview

The Start-Keep Doing-Stop survey, or SKS, is a feedback
tool for principals. It can be a part of a new principal's entry
strategy or as part of a regular feedback loop on any idea or
initiative. Respondents are asked variations of the following three
question types:

- What should we start?

- What should we keep doing?

- What should we stop?

The purpose of an SKS survey is to create direct
communication between members of the organization. SKS answers
are usually concrete examples. There are variations of this process
that rearrange the question order. Properly used, the survey can
identify areas of concern for the leader and organizational perception

about a variety of topics.

Allow respondents to remain anonymous if they desire.
Consider ending the survey with a fourth question of "Is there
anything else you would like to share with me?" Look for patterns
in the answers and follow-up with respondents who identify
themselves.

Sample SKS Questions

What Should We Start?

- What can we put in place to improve?

- What practices should we start at the campus?

- What would be beneficial for the organization to start doing?

- What are new ideas to be implemented?

What Should We Keep Doing?

- What should the Principal keep doing?

- What practices should continue?

- What has been successful that should be continued?

- What is working?

- What are people proud of at the campus?

What Should We Stop?

- What actions have been detrimental to the organization?

- Where should the Leader immediately intervene?

- What are we doing that is not working?

- What problems have not been addressed?

Appendix E

Five Points of Leadership for

Professional Beginning New

Positions

The following information was compiled by my friend and the Chief Development Officer of Life School, Charles Pulliam, after we met on the subject of entry plans for new leaders. It is his summary of some of the content and ideas of this handbook.

5 Points of Leadership for Professional Beginning New Positions

Created by Charles Pulliam and Troy Mooney

Please see the suggestions below. The items listed are helpful principles for starting a new leadership position in any industry:

1. **"Don't tear down a fence before you know why it was built"** – While you already know what you want to accomplish, take the time to learn why things are done the way they are from the people who will work for and with you prior to recommending or making changes.

2. **Seek to have individual meetings with all who work with/for you and ask the following**:
   a. Keep – What are the things you believe we are doing well and should keep doing?
   b. Stop – What are some things you believe we should stop doing?
   c. Start – What are some things you believe we should start doing?

3. **Find out in advance of your first team meeting or formal introduction about what 2-3 things that have been going well prior to your arrival**. – Use the information for your first address to the team, i.e. Thank you all for being here. I'm excited to be a part of this team. I've heard about how good you all are at "X, Y, and Z" and how well it's going… X, Y, and Z are some of the reasons I'm so excited to join the team… (Keep it short)

   a. Resist communication of planned changes, things that have been going wrong (everyone already knows), and your plan for success. There will be plenty of time for communicating change. (See item #1)

4. **Try to meet with all leaders from other areas and/or departments before you call them with a crisis or a need for help**. Some level of relationship with the leaders around you will bode well when you need help

5. **Last, but one of the most critical, involve people that work with and for you in the decisions that will impact**

them. Even if your mind is made up on what you will do, ask the people who will be impacted by your decision for input without telling them your plan. This will make them feel like a part of the process and will make "buy-in" easier.

Being the leader is so much more than position or title. It's about influence. Your ability to influence people and decisions will be equal to your success as the leader; and, it takes relationships and people to have influence. Therefore, for what it's worth, I encourage you to strongly consider and internalize the five points above. Also, remember it's often better to listen and say "I'll have to get back to you (even if you think you know the answer) prior to responding to ideas and/or making decisions about requests being made or explaining how things do or will work... Lastly, please understand most leaders don't lead as outlined above. Coincidentally, most leaders are ineffective for a season until they learn to build relationships and people and how to properly treat both.

Appendix F

Sample First Introductory Letter to Staff

Dear Champion Forest Faculty and Staff,

Please allow me the courtesy of introducing myself as the Champion Forest High School principal, Jeff Donalson. I hope you have been able to get some rest and to spend at least some of your summer doing the things you enjoy.

I am spending my time learning about Champion Forest and it is my priority to fully connect to the culture here. Making a connection, whether it is the principal with the staff or staff with the students, is the key to long term strategic success. I have time beginning July 15th through the beginning of the school year to meet with each of you. Please call the front office and schedule a time for a quick chat.

We will be working on our detailed staff development calendar which I will send to you in a second letter at a later date. Our goal is to meet district requirements but also to give you ample time to work in grade level teams in order to get ready for next year.

Champion Forest is an amazing school and we are going to have an excellent year.

Jeff Donalson

Principal

Champion Forest High School

Appendix G

Sample First Introductory Letter to

Parents

Dear parents, students, and other stakeholders,

I am indeed honored to be appointed as principal of Champion Forest High School. I feel truly blessed to be the principal of such an amazing school. I most recently served as principal of Forest Glades Middle School all right here in beautiful Champion Forest, TX. This year is going to be "Great" as we continue to provide academic experiences for our students that are rigorous, relevant, and foster great relationships. As your principal, it is important to me that everyone who steps through our doors are excited to be here! That includes, faculty, staff, students, and parents. This attitude enables us to meet the challenges of academic excellence in a positive, fun, and nurturing environment.

At Champion Forest High School we are the "Home of Champions!"
It is my desire that all of our students have that championship spirit
that has made Champion Forest High School one of the best schools
in the state of Texas. To further exemplify that spirit we need all of
our students to get involved. We have many activities, sports,
organizations, and clubs for students that appeal to a wide array of
interests. Being involved makes school fun!

Parents, we invite you to take an active role in your student's high
school career. You are a special and unique part of our learning
community. Collaboration with your student's teacher is a main
ingredient to a healthy and successful year. Open communication is
vital to ensure a successful home-school partnership throughout the
year. Parent involvement is an important aspect of every child's
education and is the primary factor in a student's success in school.

I am excited to be at Champion Forest High School. This year will
be a great year, and the best is yet to come! If I can be of assistance
please do not hesitate to call me at 555-874-8211, email me at
jdonalson@championforest.org. Go Tigers!

Sincerely,

Jeff Donalson, Jr.

Principal

Champion Forest High School

"Home of Champions"

Appendix H

Sample of Recurring Monthly Tasks

June

- Plan for campus office coverage during the summer

- Complete administrative staff evaluations

- Complete all annual checkout and year-end close-out

  procedures

- Review summer checklist for principals (see appendix)

- Begin planning for next year's staff development activities

- Complete preliminary master schedule

- Complete hiring and other personnel moves

July

- Prepare distribution for important handbooks, documents,

  and materials for students, staff, and parents

- Prepare any special plans for arrival and dismissal traffic control on first day of school
- Complete start of school professional development schedule
  - Compliance
  - Instructional
- Update master schedule
- Review staff assignments and room utilization
- Complete hiring and other personnel moves
- Plan and schedule required emergency drills
- Plan Open House
- Update web pages and social media accounts
- Update emergency contact information for faculty and staff
- Meet with team leaders and other faculty and staff
- Send out summer communication letters to staff and students
- Plan for schedule distribution to students
- Plan for identification cards, keys, etc. to be distributed
- Place all required meetings on campus calendar
- Plan pep rallies and other special campus events
- Plan for schedule change process

- Plan for resolving class size issues

- Review any grading and late work procedures

August

- Assign employee evaluation appraisers

- Conduct readiness checks for start of school

  o Team meetings scheduled

  o Faculty meetings scheduled

  o Parent Teacher Organization meetings scheduled

  o Duty schedule created

  o Substitute plans and procedures ready

  o Instructional materials distributed

  o Maintenance issues complete

  o Rooms have appropriate chairs and desks

- Ensure public address and bell systems are functioning

- Plan for responding to dress code infractions

- Check on class size balance

- Plan Open House

September

- Continue planning Open House

- Plan for monitoring student academic performance

- Monitor:

    o Student and staff attendance

    o Fundraisers

    o Bullying and investigations

    o Grades

- Complete required drills

October

- Prepare for Daylight Savings changeover and adjusting building and parking lighting schedules

- Remind students to make good choices

- Plan for Halloween

- Complete required drills

November

- Prepare for custody issues over long school breaks

- Complete required drills

- Begin plans for January professional development

- Plan schedules for final semester exams if applicable

- Complete required drills

- Plan for holiday parties and celebrations

December

- Finalize plans for professional development in January

- Write cards or notes to staff for Christmas

- Complete required drills

- Finalize plan for 1st day back with staff and students

- Prepare for custody issues over long school breaks

- Plan for schedule distribution for new semester

January

- Review campus student intervention plans

    o Review all semester grades

        ▪ Look at success rates by teacher

- Monitor Senior transcripts and adjust classes as needed
- Continue to monitor
  - Student and staff attendance
  - Fundraisers
  - Bullying and investigations
  - Grades
- Review staff evaluation progress to date
- Complete required drills

February

- Plan for summer professional development
- Remind campuses to plan for Valentine's Day and deliveries
  - Create holding area and ensure accurate method of recording deliveries
  - Schedule deliveries for certain times of the day
- Complete required drills

March

- Check on progress of teacher evaluations

- Review any spring break procedures or monitoring

- Remind students to make good choices

- Review supervision of events

- Be highly visible during lunches

- Be highly visible during transition

- Review Seniors at risk of not graduating

- Complete required drills

- Plan for end of the year celebrations and recognitions

- Notify parents of potential failures

- Begin interviewing for any personnel vacancies for following school year

April

- Review plans for selecting summer school attendees

- Set dates for Master Schedule planning meetings

- Plan teacher appreciation week

- Prepare end of year checklists

- Collect summer vacation schedules for administrative staff

- Continue interviewing for any personnel vacancies for following school year

May

- Plan for grade collection and final review of grade submissions
- Plan for collection of all instructional materials
- Remind students to make good choices
- Review plans for any summer retesting for statewide assessments
- Review plans for summer maintenance
- Schedule Administrative evaluations
- Plan for employee checkout
- Plan for student locker cleanout
- Update teacher contact information

Ready to Lead: An Entry Guide for New Principals

Produced April 2017

Troy Mooney

Email: Troy.mooney@lifeschools.net

Twitter: @troymooney

Facebook: https://www.facebook.com/troymooneyblog/

Website: www.troymooney.com

Herbert O'Neil

Email: Herbert.oneil@lifeschools.net

Twitter: @herbertoneiljr

Website: www.herbertoneil.com

Made in the USA
Columbia, SC
02 February 2018